Michael Bojesen

Eternity

Lyrics: Ellen Heiberg
(transl.: Lisa Freeman)

for chorus (SATB) and piano

EDITION WILHELM HANSEN

Eternity

Music: Michael Bojesen
Lyrics: Ellen Heiberg
Transl.: Lisa Freeman

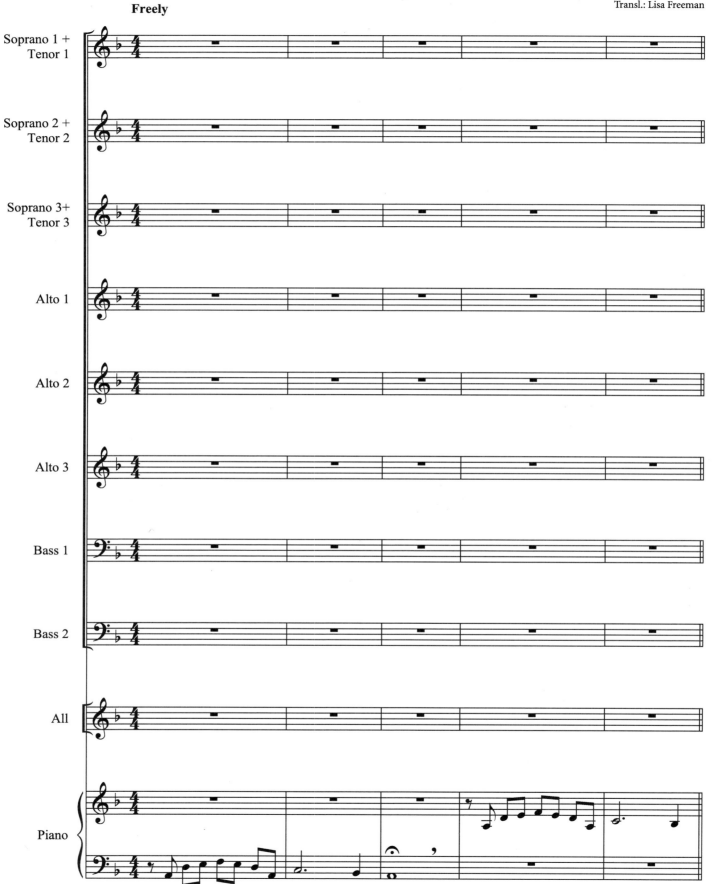

lands.

Hide it in your poc - ket where oth - er eyes can't see, _____

it's your piece___ of the o - cean and all e - ter - ni - ty. _____

WH31243 · Eternity

WH31243 · Eternity

WH31243 · Eternity